The future belongs to those who believe in the beauty of their dreams.

— Marie Curie

Always Believe in Yourself and Your Dreams

A Collection from Blue Mountain Arts®
Edited by Patricia Wayant

Blue Mountain Press®

Boulder, Colorado

Copyright © 1997, 1999 by Stephen Schutz and Susan Polis Schutz.
Copyright © 1997, 1999 by Blue Mountain Arts, Inc.

Library of Congress Catalog Card Number: 99-24383
ISBN: 0-88396-513-5

ACKNOWLEDGMENTS appear on page 64.

 design on book cover is registered in the U.S. Patent and Trademark Office.

Manufactured in Korea
Second Printing in Hardcover: December 1999

Library of Congress Cataloging-in-Publication Data

Always believe in yourself and your dreams : a collection from Blue
    Mountain Arts / edited by Patricia Wayant.
        p.   cm.
    ISBN 0-88396-513-5 (alk. paper)
    1. Self-actualization (Psychology) Poetry. 2. American poetry--20th
century. 3. Success Poetry. I. Wayant, Patricia, 1953-
PS595.S45A49   1999
808.81'9353--dc21   99-24383
                                                                          CIP

Blue Mountain Press INC.

P.O. Box 4549, Boulder, Colorado 80306

Table of Contents

Don't Ever Doubt
Yourself

You have so much to offer,
so much to give, and so much
you deserve to receive in return.
Don't ever doubt that.
Know yourself and all of your fine
qualities.
Rejoice in all your marvelous strengths
of mind and body.
Be glad for the virtues that are yours,
and pat yourself on the back for all
your many admirable achievements.

Keep positive.
Concentrate on that which
makes you happy,
and build yourself up.
Stay nimble of heart,
happy of thought,
healthy of mind, and
well in being.

— Janet A. Sullivan

Your Life Holds Unlimited Potential

You have the ability
to attain whatever you seek;
within you is every potential
you can imagine.
Always aim higher than
you believe you can reach.
So often, you'll discover
that when your talents
are set free
by your imagination,
you can achieve any goal.
If people offer
their help or wisdom
as you go through life,
accept it gratefully.
You can learn much from those
who have gone before you.

Never be afraid or hesitant
to step off the accepted path
and head in your own direction
if your heart tells you
that it's the right way for you.
Always believe that you will
ultimately succeed
at whatever you do,
and never forget the value
of persistence, discipline,
and determination.
You are meant to be
whatever you dream
of becoming.

— Edmund O'Neill

You Deserve
a Life of Happiness

You will get only what you seek
Choose your goals carefully
Know what you like
and what you do not like
Be critical about what you can do well
and what you cannot do well
Choose a career or lifestyle that interests you
and work hard to make it a success
but also have fun in what you do
Be honest with people
   and help them if you can
but don't depend on anyone
   to make life easy or happy for you
(only you can do that for yourself)
Be strong and decisive
but remain sensitive
Regard your family, and the idea of family
as the basis for security, support and love
Understand who you are
and what you want in life
before sharing your life with someone
When you are ready to enter a relationship
make sure that the person is worthy of
everything you are physically and mentally
Strive to achieve your dreams
Find happiness in everything you do
Love with your entire being
Love with an uninhibited soul
Make a triumph
of every aspect
of your life

— Susan Polis Schutz

Twelve Ways to Keep Smiling!

*H*old on to your dreams, and
never let them go ⟿ Show the rest
of the world how wonderful you are!
⟿ Give circumstances a chance, and
give others the benefit of the doubt
⟿ Wish on a star that shines in
your sky ⟿ Take on your problems
one by one and work things out ⟿
Rely on all the strength you have
inside ⟿ Let loose of the sparkle
and spirit that you sometimes try
to hide ⟿ Stay in touch with those
who touch your life with love ⟿
Look on the bright side and don't
let adversity keep you from winning
⟿ Be yourself, because you are filled
with special qualities that have
brought you this far, and that will
always see you through ⟿ Keep your
spirits up ⟿ Make your heart happy,
and let it reflect on everything you do!

— Douglas Pagels

The Power of Change
Is in Your Hands

Life is a set of circumstances that
you can change, improve,
and make better day by day.
It's your decision; it's in your hands.
Just like the potter at the wheel,
you are the force that turns and moves
the clay into a thing of beauty.
Like the painter's brush depicting
something fresh and new and picturesque,
you can create the scenery that's best
for you.

Each person has the power to take
control of every circumstance in life —
to change, improve,
and make it better day by day.
Not one of us can say:
"I must accept whatever comes my way,"
because the way we choose to go
through life is our decision.
The power of change is always
in your hands.

— Barbara J. Hall

Believe in Miracles!

Love your life.
Believe in your own power,
   your own potential,
      and your own innate goodness.
Every morning, wake with the awe
   of just being alive.
Each day, discover the magnificent,
   awesome beauty in the world.
Explore and embrace life in yourself
   and in everyone you see each day.
Reach within to find your own specialness.
Amaze yourself,
   and rouse those around you
      to the potential of each new day.
Don't be afraid to admit
   that you are less than perfect;
      this is the essence of your humanity.
Let those who love you help you.
Trust enough to be able to take.
Look with hope to the horizon of today,
   for today is all we truly have.
Live this day well.
Let a little sunshine out as well as in.
Create your own rainbows.
Be open to all your possibilities;
   possibilities can be miracles.
Always believe in miracles!

— Vickie M. Worsham

*Let nothing hold you back from
      exploring your wildest fantasies,
         wishes, and aspirations.
Don't be afraid to dream big
and to follow your dreams
   wherever they may lead you.
Open your eyes to their beauty;
open your mind to their magic;
open your heart to their possibilities.
Only by dreaming will you ever discover
who you are, what you want,
   and what you can do.
Don't be afraid to take risks,
   to become involved,
   to make a commitment.
Do whatever it takes to make
   your dreams come true.
Always believe in miracles,
   and always believe in you!*

— Julie Anne Ford

Create Your Own World

*Every day has
its own rewards
and its own unique challenges.
None of us has
the same exact worries
or responsibilities,
because life is shaped
around each of us as individuals.
It's important to remember that
we all create our own worlds.
Who we are and the way we act
are how we control our lives.
There are endless opportunities
for us to change and rearrange
the day-to-day moments
  we are given.
It's up to each of us to decide
which way we want to go;
how far or how fast
we go in life are the choices
we all must make for ourselves.*

— Dena Dilaconi

It's Up to You

This life is the only one
you're given.
Look for opportunities to grow,
and never be discouraged
in your efforts to do so.
Replace your weaknesses
with positives;
take life's broken pieces
and re-create your dreams.
Never measure the future
by the past;
let yesterday become a memory
and tomorrow a promise.

Begin each day by focusing
on all that is good,
and you'll be in a position
to handle whatever comes along.
Take responsibility for
your actions;
never make excuses
for not being the best
you can be.
If you should slip,
be comforted by the thought
that we all do at times.
Determine your tomorrow
by the choices you make today,
and you'll find yourself living
in joy and triumph.

— *Linda E. Knight*

The Secret to Life
Is Living It
One Day at a Time

*O*ur lives are made up of a million
moments, spent in a million different ways.
Some are spent searching for love, peace, and
harmony. Others are spent surviving day to day.
But there is no greater moment than when we
find that life, with all its joys and sorrows, is
meant to be lived one day at a time.

It's in this knowledge that we discover the
most wonderful truth of all. Whether we live in
a forty-room mansion, surrounded by servants
and wealth, or find it a struggle to manage the
rent month to month, we have it within our
power to be fully satisfied and live a life with
true meaning.

One day at a time — we have that ability,
through cherishing each moment and rejoicing
in each dream. We can experience each day anew,
and with this fresh start we have what it takes
to make all of our dreams come true. Each day
is new, and living one day at a time enables us
to truly enjoy life and live it to the fullest.

— Regina Hill

Never Let Go of Hope

*One day
you will see
that it all
has finally come together.*

*What you have
always wished for
has finally come to be.*

*You will look back
and laugh at what has passed
and you will ask yourself,
"How did I get through all of that?"*

*Just
never let go of hope.
Just
never quit dreaming.
And
never let love
depart from your life.*

— jancarl campi

The Path to a Dream

The path to a dream is paved
  with sacrifices
and lined with determination.
And though it has many stumbling blocks
  along the way
and may go in more than one direction,
  it is marked with faith.
It is traveled by belief and courage,
  persistence and hard work.
It is conquered with a willingness
to face challenges and take chances,
  to fail and try again and again.
Along the way, you may have to confront
  doubts, setbacks, and unfairness.
But when the path comes to an end,
you will find that there is no greater joy
than making your dream come true.

— Barbara Cage

Just Be Yourself

To be who you are
is to be enough.
To share who you are
is to share enough.
To do what you love
is to do enough.

There is no race to win
and nothing to be proven,
only dreams to be nurtured,
a self to be expressed,
and love to be shared.

Never doubt your worth,
and always know,
without any doubt,
that you are truly valued.

— *Donna Newman*

Make the Most of Every Day, and Celebrate All That You Are

Live by your own light ⤎ Shine by your own star ⤎ Do what you always wanted to do with your life ⤎ Envision the gift that you are ⤎ Climb up the hills of your hopes and dreams ⤎ Take whatever steps you need to take ⤎ You can't get to the top if you don't try, and it's a journey you should definitely make ⤎

Try to find more time in your life ⤎ Do it just for you ⤎ The people you love and care about will be rewarded with your happiness, too ⤎ When the calendar is far too full ⤎ Keep the days from flying by ⤎ Remember your youth when time took forever ⤎ Rediscover that child inside ⤎

Spend part of every day just doing something you'd like to do ⤝ *Today will never come again, and yesterday is through* ⤝ *The secret (if you'd like to know) to finding happiness* ⤝ *Is knowing that it's all around and that your life is blessed* ⤝ *By being in this moment and living a day at a time* ⤝ *You have access to every gift that will make your sunlight shine* ⤝ *Brighten your world with friendships and love and wishes on a star* ⤝

Make the most of every day ⤝ *And celebrate all that you are* ⤝

— Douglas Pagels

Never Let Go of the Dreams in Your Heart

Sometimes it seems that our dreams
Crumble in our hands.
We think that we have failed
And that all we tried
So hard to attain
Will now always stay
Slightly out of reach.

But one failure cannot
Crumble the dreams
That years of hard work
And dedication have built.
So hold on to your dreams.
Believe in yourself,
And you will find that a
Bright tomorrow
Waits just around the next turn.
You will make it.
You will be successful.
And your dream will come true...
Just keep believing!

— Jennifer Eller

Be Strong,
and Don't Give Up

Remember... there is a deeper strength
and an amazing abundance of peace
available to you.
Draw from this well;
call on your faith to uphold you.
Life continues around us,
even when our troubles seem to stop time.
There is always good in life.
Take a few minutes to distract yourself
from your concerns —
long enough to draw strength from a tree
or to find pleasure in a bird's song.
Return a smile;
realize that life is a series of levels,
cycles of ups and downs —
some easy, some challenging.
Through it all, we learn;
we grow strong in faith;
we mature in understanding.
The difficult times are often
the best teachers, and there is
good to be found in all situations.
Reach for the good.
Be strong, and don't give up.

— Pamela Owens Renfro

To Get What You Want
Out of Life...

*It takes believing in your dreams
and in what you know to be true.
Surviving disappointments
and the times when
    you're truly alone.
Awakening to see that you
    have made it through
the difficult times
with only yourself to depend on.
It takes facing the truth
that only you can shape your destiny.
Realizing that the footsteps
    you take today
are the ones that will
    lead you into tomorrow,
and they must be guided by
    an unswerving faith in yourself.
Understanding that the failures,
    setbacks, and hurts
life often gives us all
only serve as steppingstones
    to true happiness —
and if you follow the trail
instead of turning back,
only then will you recognize
    your strengths
and be able to view life
    from the summit.*

— Debra McCleary

Know Yourself

Know what you can
and want to do in life
Set goals for yourself
and work hard to achieve them
Strive to have fun every day
Use your creativity as a means
of expressing your feelings
Be sensitive
in viewing the world
Develop a sense of confidence
Be honest with yourself
and with others
Follow your heart
and adhere to your own truths
Know that the more you give
the more you will receive
Believe in yourself
and your dreams
will come true

— Susan Polis Schutz

*Whatever you can do,
or dream you can... begin it.
Boldness has genius, power
and magic in it.*

— Johann Wolfgang von Goethe

*To accomplish great things,
we must not only act,
but also dream,
not only plan,
but also believe.*

— Anatole France

*Nothing can bring you peace
but yourself.*

— Ralph Waldo Emerson

Success Has
No Limits...

There are no limits
to what you can do.
Your talents and abilities,
your uniqueness and warmth,
your strength and dedication
in everything you do —
all of these will help you
reach your dreams.

There are no limits
to what life has to offer you.
The world is full of possibilities,
just as you are filled with promise.
Seek, discover, and embrace with openness
the richness of experience.
Believe in yourself,
and you will always know success.

— Michelle Richards

Let Your Heart
Show You the Way

Listen
to the song in you.
It's there
in whatever puts stars
in your eyes
and makes your heart sing.
Listen
to your feelings
and you will hear
who you are
and what you must do.
Listen
to your needs
and you will know
where to find
what you are looking for.

Listen
  to the wisdom within.
  It is trying to lead you
  to your destiny.
Listen
  to the song in you
  and your life
  will be full of harmony.
  You will be
  who you were meant to be.
  You will be complete
  and at peace
  and happier than you
  have ever been —
  if only you will
Listen
  to the song in you.

— Nancye Sims

If You're Struggling
Over a Difficult Decision...

My best advice to you is to give it "the rocking chair test." Imagine that you're ninety years old, sitting on the porch and rocking in your chair as you reflect back on your life. Will you regret doing this — or _not_ doing it? Pick the decision you can live with, and have no regrets in your choice. Believe in the choices you make.

— Anne Larnella Hood

When the task at hand
is a mountain
in front of you...

When the task at hand is a mountain
in front of you
it may seem too hard to climb.
But you don't have to climb it
all at once —
just one step at a time.
Take one small step...
and one small step...
then another...
and you'll find...
the task at hand that was a mountain
in front of you...

> *...is a mountain*
> *you have climbed.*

— Ashley Rice

Difficult Times
Don't Last Forever

Sometimes, the problems
you must face
are more than you wish
to cope with,
and tomorrow doesn't seem
to offer any solutions.

You may ask yourself "Why me?"
but the answer is sometimes unclear.
You may even tend to feel
that life hasn't been just or fair
to burden you with such obstacles.

The roads any of us choose
to follow are never free
of bumps or curves,
but eventually the turns
lead to a smoother path ahead.

Believe in yourself and your dreams.
You will soon realize that
the future holds many promises
for you.
Remember... difficult times
don't last forever.

— *Geri Danks*

A Creed for Being the Best You Can Be

Speak and you will be heard;
  make your words kind
    and you will be judged so.
Love kindly and unselfishly,
  with no wish to possess.
Search for who you are
  and for what matters.
Give freely to all,
  and you shall receive
    so much more.
Listen to the troubles of others,
  and your own shall be halved.
Live each day as your last,
  treasuring each sight and sound.
Accept what you have
  and all that is freely given.
Strive to be greater than
  you were before.
Ask, and even your smallest wish
  will be granted.
Dream of what can be —
  a world of peace and beauty
    for all to share.

— Stephanie Robinson

You Are Capable
of Tremendous Achievements!

*Know what you are capable of,
and believe that it's more
     than what you're doing now.*

*Visualize yourself at
     your ultimate best,
and see yourself living
     any dream that comes your way.*

*Believe that you can make
     your dreams come true,
and that patience and determination
     will see them through.*

Care enough to make the sacrifices
  it takes,
and don't let the present have
  priority over the future.

Know that having a good time
  can include learning
    and growing,
and that there is joy in creating
  and succeeding.

Realize what a talented
  and unique person you are,
and that happiness comes
  when you challenge yourself...
    and win!

— *Barbara Cage*

Trust in Yourself

I believe all of us have a built-in compass to help us get to wherever we desire to go. Don't forget to trust that compass, and refer to it often, for with that trusting will come the strength to bear whatever life deals you.

Don't get led astray. Ask your heart for the truth, and it will come up with the answer and the good judgment to make the decisions you'll need to make. Love everyone, and don't question love's reception. Do the best you can. Live each day as it comes. We can't get ahead of ourselves anyway.

Remember: just as you have questions now, somewhere inside you, and down the road, there will be better answers and workable solutions. It takes patience and trust to get through life's changes when you're trying to reach goals, solve problems, and make dreams come true. Though at times it may seem more than you can take, I know you are strong, and you can handle whatever comes your way. Trust in yourself.

— *Donna Fargo*

Only You Can Make the Right Things Happen in Your Life

You don't need anyone else
to give your life direction.
You know what's right for you.
Inside your heart exists
a special knowledge
of the plans you've made,
the hopes you have,
and the dreams you hold.
You may be hesitant at times,
even fearful to go on,
but that's a natural feeling
all of us go through.
What you need to remember
is what means the most to you
and how to keep alive your hopes
and dreams.
Then, with all the greatness
that is within you,
go in that new direction —
backed by your own faith,
decisive courage,
and a heart filled with dreams.
And remember that only you
can make the right things
happen in your life.

— Barbara J. Hall

This is how it works.

Each new day is a blank page in the diary of your life. The pen is in your hand, but the lines will not all be written the way you choose; some will come from the world and the circumstances that surround you.

But for the many things that <u>are</u> in your control, there is something special you need to know...

The secret of life is in making your story as beautiful as it can be. Write the diary of your days and fill the pages with words that come from the heart. As the pages take you through time, you will discover paths that will add to your happiness and your sorrows, but if you can do these things, there will always be hope in your tomorrows.

Follow your dreams. Work hard. Be kind. This is all anyone could ever ask: Do what you can to make the door open on a day... that is filled with beauty in some special way. Remember: Goodness will be rewarded. Smiles will pay you back. Have fun. Find strength. Be truthful. Have faith. Don't focus on the things you lack.

Realize that people are the treasures in life — and happiness is the real wealth. Have a diary that describes how you did your best, and...

The rest will take care of itself.

— *Douglas Pagels*

The Strength of
the Human Spirit

Dreams come true because someone believes they can, and without thought of failure, they risk everything they have within them.

Hopes are always renewed because someone won't give up, and they don't allow the risks involved to keep them from taking a chance.

Wishes that seem so impossible can be wished for anyway, and they will come into reality because of simple faith.

Faith is the one thing in life that can take you through any pain, relieve any worry or sorrow, and keep you believing in the joys of tomorrow.

Faith is the ability to believe in the idea that good will eventually come from the worst possible situation, pain, or disillusionment.

It carries us through bad times with a deep sense of security and strength, and the knowledge that whatever might come, we possess the ability to overcome any obstacle, overlook obvious discouragements, and keep on trying through any disappointment.

Faith is the one thing in life that you'll always need, because the strength you possess... is the strength of the human spirit.

— *Regina Hill*

Don't Give Up

Even when you get a little discouraged, don't allow yourself to give up. Only when you have done your very best can you stop and say to yourself, "I tried," and that's what matters most.

If you back away from obstacles that appear before you because they seem too difficult, then you're not being true to yourself. Don't be afraid to take risks, or even to fail. It isn't about winning or losing. It's about loving yourself enough and believing in who you are that counts in the end.

Throughout your life, you will undoubtedly face challenges that may try your patience. Just remember that it is <u>you</u> who will always come out ahead, as long as you know in your heart that you did the best you could and that's all that really matters.

— *T. Nash*

Be a Dreamer

Dare to dream,
  for dreamers see tomorrow.
Dare to make a wish,
  for wishing makes way for hope,
and hope is what keeps
  us all alive.
Dare to reach out
for the things no one else can see.
Be unafraid to see what
  others cannot.
Believe in your heart
  and in your own goodness,
for in doing so
  others will believe
    in them, too.
Believe in magic,
  because life is full of it.
But most of all,
  believe in yourself...
because within you lies
  all of the magic,
the hope, the love,
and the dreams of tomorrow.

— *Ron Cristian*

Live Your Life
with Courage

Courage is admitting that you're afraid and facing that fear directly. It's being strong enough to ask for help and humble enough to accept it.

Courage is standing up for what you believe in without worrying about the opinions of others. It's following your own heart, living your own life, and settling for nothing less than the best for yourself.

Courage is daring to take a first step, a big leap, or a different path. It's attempting to do something that no one has done before, and all others thought impossible.

Courage is keeping heart in the face of disappointment, and looking at defeat not as an end but as a new beginning. It's believing that things will ultimately get better even as they get worse.

Courage is being responsible for your own actions, and admitting your own mistakes without placing blame on others. It's relying not on others for your success, but on your own skills and efforts.

Courage is refusing to quit even when you're intimidated by impossibility. It's choosing a goal, sticking with it, and finding solutions to the problems.

Courage is thinking big, aiming high, and shooting far. It's taking a dream and doing anything, risking everything, and stopping at nothing to make it a reality.

— *Caroline Kent*

Do Whatever You Need to Do...

If need be, go it alone —
your victory will be even sweeter.
If need be, go slowly —
how fast you get there
isn't important.
If need be, start over
   again and again —
success becomes closer each time.
If need be, accept whatever
   you have to —
it may not be easy to do,
but it makes everything easier.
If need be, stop running —
so that happiness can find you.
If need be, admit that
   you need help —
this is helping yourself.
If need be, ignore fear —
for without fear,
   anything is possible.
If need be, make a change —
it could change your life.
If need be, surrender —
without struggle, there is peace.
If need be, compromise —
but keep your principles.

If need be, continue
what seems to be impossible —
it only is impossible if you quit.
If need be, stop —
and a new life will start.
If need be, try something different —
you will be wiser.
If need be, wait —
amazing things happen every day.
If need be, live with uncertainty —
certainty is in trusting yourself.
If need be, have faith —
and faithfully you'll be given
strength.
If need be, go forward —
your dreams are waiting
patiently for you.

— Nancye Sims

There Is Only One Key to Success: Never Quit!

Believe in yourself
and your vision of the future.
Surround yourself with
those who believe in you
and will help you achieve
your goals.
Keep your dream alive
despite the challenges
along the way.

There will always be those
who try to steal your dream
by laughter or criticism.
They cannot understand what
drives you to always want more.

In safety, there is no failure —
neither is there success.
Only by taking the risks
that others fear
can you achieve greatness.

Change can be frightening,
but only by changing
can you experience growth.
Only by challenging yourself
to do what seems impossible
can you ever know how much
you can achieve.

There is only one key
to success:
never quit until you win.
It may require a lot of changing,
but you can do it.
The seed of greatness
lies within you.
Nurture it, and there
will be nothing you can't do.

— Lisa Marie Yost

*Do not wish to be anything
but what you are,
and try to be that perfectly.*

— St. Francis de Sales

*Be what you are,
and become
what you are capable
of becoming.*

— Robert Louis Stevenson

Always Believe in Yourself and Your Dreams

Believe in what makes you feel good.
Believe in what makes you happy.
Believe in the dreams
 you've always wanted to come true,
 and give them every chance to.
Life holds no promises
 as to what will come your way.
You must search for your own ideals
 and work toward reaching them.
Life makes no guarantees
 as to what you'll have.
It just gives you time to make choices
 and to take chances
and to discover whatever secrets
 that might come your way.
If you are willing to take
 the opportunities you are given
 and utilize the abilities you have,
you will constantly fill your life
 with special moments
 and unforgettable times.
No one knows the mysteries of life
 or its ultimate meaning,
but for those who are willing
 to believe in their dreams
 and in themselves,
life is a precious gift
 in which anything is possible.

— Dena Dilaconi

You Can Design
Your Own Destiny

You are a wonderful person,
so do wonderful things.
You can make a difference
in your world.
You have a purpose;
you have the power;
you are magic.
You can create beauty,
recall the past,
plan the future.
You can soar in imagination.
You have the courage to question,
and you can choose to change.
The only limitations you have
are those in your own mind;
don't be satisfied with less than
all you can be.
Don't compare yourself with others;
draw your own dreams
and design your own destiny.
Live each day to the fullest.
Give a little more than you take.
Make this world a better place to live,
and always — always —
listen to your own heart,
for only you know what is best for you.

— *Vickie M. Worsham*

May There Never Be a Dream That Is Beyond Your Reach

May there be no dead ends in your life
and no roads traveled
  without blessings.
May no day be too short
  to fit love and laughter into it;
may time never be so scarce
  that you cannot give yourself
some quiet and gentle thoughts.
May there be no friends too busy for you
and no family member
  who doesn't greatly love you.

May there never be a dream
  beyond your reach
or a star that you are unable to touch
once you get started on your journey.
May you remember all
  you have had from the start
and all that is yours forever.

— Mary Klock Labdon

Dreams Come True
One Step at a Time

When going through life
and traveling in the direction
of your dreams, the best way
to get ahead is the simplest way:

Take it one step at a time.

Don't look over your shoulder; if you do,
you'll feel the weight of all your
yesterdays upon you.
And don't worry about what lies ahead.
By the time you get to
the bend in the road
or the crest of the hill,
you're going to be better and stronger
than you ever were before.

Just go a step at a time,
one day at a time.
And you'll find a rich, thankful life
you never thought you could afford.

— A. Rogers

Promise Yourself

Promise yourself that you'll always remember what a special person you are ⇐ Promise yourself that you'll hold on to your hopes and reach out for your stars ⇐ Promise yourself that you'll live with happiness over the years and over the miles ⇐ Promise yourself that you'll "remember when..." and you'll always "look forward to..." ⇐ Promise yourself that you'll do the things you have always wanted to do ⇐ Promise yourself that you'll cherish your dreams as treasures you have kept ⇐ Promise yourself that you'll enjoy life day by day and step by step ⇐ Promise yourself a life of love and joy and all your dreams come true ⇐

— *Collin McCarty*

Always Create Your Own Dreams and Live Life to the Fullest

*D*reams can come true
if you take the time to
think about what you want in life
Get to know yourself
Find out who you are
Choose your goals carefully
Be honest with yourself
Always believe in yourself
Find many interests and pursue them
Find out what is important to you
Find out what you are good at
Don't be afraid to make mistakes
Work hard to achieve successes

When things are not going right
don't give up — just try harder
Give yourself freedom
* to try out new things*
Laugh and have a good time
Open yourself up to love
Take part in the beauty of nature
Be appreciative of all that you have
Help those less fortunate than you
Work towards peace in the world
Live life to the fullest
Create your own dreams and
follow them until they are a reality

— Susan Polis Schutz

Don't Ever Forget That You Are Special

Don't ever forget that you are unique.
Be your best self
and not an imitation of someone else.
Find your strengths
and use them in a positive way.
Don't listen to those
who ridicule the choices you make.
Travel the road that you have chosen
and don't look back with regret.
You have to take chances
to make your dreams happen.
Remember that there is plenty of time
to travel another road — and still another —
in your journey through life.
Take the time to find the route
that is right for you.

You will learn something valuable
from every trip you take,
so don't be afraid to make mistakes.
Tell yourself that you're okay
just the way you are.
Make friends who respect your true self.
Take the time to be alone, too,
so you can know just how terrific
your own company can be.
Remember that being alone
doesn't always mean being lonely;
it can be a beautiful experience
of finding your creativity,
your heartfelt feelings,
and the calm and quiet peace deep inside you.
Don't ever forget that you are special.

— Jacqueline Schiff

Follow Your Destiny, Wherever It Leads You

*T*here comes a time in your life when you realize that if you stand still, you will remain at this point forever. You realize that if you fall and stay down, life will pass you by.

Life's circumstances are not always what you might wish them to be. The pattern of life does not necessarily go as you plan. Beyond any understanding, you may at times be led in different directions that you never imagined, dreamed, or designed. Yet if you had never put any effort into choosing a path, or tried to carry out your dream, then perhaps you would have no direction at all.

Rather than wondering about or questioning the direction your life has taken, accept the fact that there is a path before you now. Shake off the "why's" and "what if's," and rid yourself of confusion. Whatever was — is in the past. Whatever is — is what's important. The past is a brief reflection. The future is yet to be realized. Today is here.

Walk your path one step at a time — with courage, faith, and determination. Keep your head up, and cast your dreams to the stars. Soon your steps will become firm and your footing will be solid again. A path that you never imagined will become the most comfortable direction you could have ever hoped to follow.

Keep your belief in yourself and walk into your new journey. You will find it magnificent, spectacular, and beyond your wildest imaginings.

— Vicki Silvers

ACKNOWLEDGMENTS

The following is a partial list of authors and authors' representatives whom the publisher especially wishes to thank for permission to reprint their works.

PrimaDonna Entertainment Corp. for "Trust in Yourself" by Donna Fargo. Copyright © 1997 by PrimaDonna Entertainment Corp. All rights reserved. Reprinted by permission.

Barbara J. Hall for "The Power of Change Is in Your Hands." Copyright © 1997 by Barbara J. Hall. And for "Only You Can Make the Right Things Happen in Your Life." Copyright © 1999 by Barbara J. Hall. All rights reserved. Reprinted by permission.

Dena Dilaconi for "Create Your Own World." Copyright © 1997 by Dena Dilaconi. All rights reserved. Reprinted by permission.

Regina Hill for "The Secret to Life Is Living It One Day at a Time." Copyright © 1997 by Regina Hill. And for "The Strength of the Human Spirit." Copyright © 1999 by Regina Hill. All rights reserved. Reprinted by permission.

jancarl campi for "Never Let Go of Hope." Copyright © 1997 by jancarl campi. All rights reserved. Reprinted by permission.

Donna Newman for "Just Be Yourself." Copyright © 1997 by Donna Newman. All rights reserved. Reprinted by permission.

Jennifer Eller for "Never Let Go of the Dreams in Your Heart." Copyright © 1997 by Jennifer Eller. All rights reserved. Reprinted by permission.

Pamela Owens Renfro for "Be Strong and Don't Give Up." Copyright © 1997 by Pamela Owens Renfro. All rights reserved. Reprinted by permission.

Debra McCleary for "To Get What You Want Out of Life...." Copyright © 1997 by Debra McCleary. All rights reserved. Reprinted by permission.

Michelle Richards for "Success Has No Limits." Copyright © 1997 by Michelle Richards. All rights reserved. Reprinted by permission.

Nancye Sims for "Let Your Heart Show You the Way" and "Do Whatever You Need to Do...." Copyright © 1997 by Nancye Sims. All rights reserved. Reprinted by permission.

Anne Larnella Hood for "If You're Struggling Over a Difficult Decision...." Copyright © 1997 by Anne Larnella Hood. All rights reserved. Reprinted by permission.

Stephanie Robinson for "A Creed for Being the Best You Can Be." Copyright © 1997 by Stephanie Robinson. All rights reserved. Reprinted by permission.

Barbara Cage for "You Are Capable of Tremendous Achievements!" Copyright © 1999 by Barbara Cage. All rights reserved. Reprinted by permission.

T. Nash for "Don't Give Up." Copyright © 1999 by T. Nash. All rights reserved. Reprinted by permission.

Caroline Kent for "Live Your Life with Courage." Copyright © 1997 by Caroline Kent. All rights reserved. Reprinted by permission.

Lisa Marie Yost for "There Is Only One Key to Success: Never Quit!" Copyright © 1997 by Lisa Marie Yost. All rights reserved. Reprinted by permission.

Vickie M. Worsham for "You Can Design Your Own Destiny." Copyright © 1997 by Vickie M. Worsham. All rights reserved. Reprinted by permission.

A careful effort has been made to trace the ownership of poems used in this anthology in order to obtain permission to reprint copyrighted materials and give proper credit to the copyright owners. If any error or omission has occurred, it is completely inadvertent, and we would like to make corrections in future editions provided that written notification is made to the publisher:

BLUE MOUNTAIN PRESS, INC., P.O. Box 4549, Boulder, Colorado 80306.